Weather

KINGFISHER

First published 2012 by Kingfisher
an imprint of Macmillan Children's Books
a division of Macmillan Publishers Limited
20 New Wharf Road, London N1 9RR
Basingstoke and Oxford
Associated companies throughout the world
www.panmacmillan.com

ISBN 978-0-7534-3252-5

Consultant: Dr Peter Inness, University of Reading

Designed and created by Basher www.basherbooks.com
Text written by Dan Green

Dedicated to Simon Marbrook
Text and design copyright © Toucan Books Ltd. 2012
Based on an original concept by Toucan Books Ltd.
Illustrations copyright © Simon Basher 2012

9 8 7 6 5 4 3 2 1
1TR/0512/WKT/UG/140MA

A CIP catalogue record for this book
is available from the British Library.

Printed in China

CONTENTS

Introduction   4
World of Weather   6
Blue-sky Dreamers   22
Wet 'n' Wild   34
Extreme Weather   46
Index   60
Glossary   62

Introduction

Weather

Whatever weather you're having right now, it is bound to be the subject of conversation. People just love to talk about the weather! Did you know that there are some places on this planet where the weather doesn't change much from day to day? People living there wake up and pull on the same kinds of clothing every morning. Yet in other places, not only is the weather variable from one day to the next, but it can even change dramatically in the course of 24 hours! First it's sunny, then it's rainy, then it's windy, then it's rainy again… In these places folk need an entire wardrobe of clothes and a suitcase of gear just to get from one end of the day to the other!

One thing that seems certain about this weather of ours (apart from the fact that it's tricky to forecast) is that it is changing. That's right! In your lifetime the weather is going to get very interesting indeed. There are things happening with the world's climates right now, and the Extreme Weather crew are trying to get more of a look-in. You need to get to know these guys, and their fair-weather friends. Come on, let's meet them.

Weather

Chapter 1
World of Weather

This powerful bunch has taken the world by storm. A few of these high rollers have an impact that influences the entire planet, and many of them are large-scale weather systems. The Sun is the boss, as its energy makes all of Earth's weather. Yearly cycles, such as the Seasons, Monsoon and (to a lesser extent) El Niño are created by the angle at which the planet orbits the Sun. The tilt is so great that, in winter, the poles remain constantly in Earth's shadow, facing away from Sun, and so receive no sunlight. In summer, the reverse is true: polar regions become "lands of the midnight sun" and have no night.

Sun

Seasons

Climate

Monsoon

El Niño

Forecast

Weather
Satellite

Climate
Change

Sun

■ World of Weather

☀ The centre of the Solar System, this dude is our nearest star
☀ Provides energy to drive climate, weather and life on Earth
☀ This early riser shines a bright light that we call "day"

G'day! I am the brightest thing in the sky. I dazzle when Earth turns on its axis to face me and I outshine everything. I have the power to make you smile, I can even make you take your clothes off! But that's nothing compared to the dizzying effects I have on gassy Atmosphere.

I'm simply bursting with energy – visible light, radio and infrared waves, ultraviolet waves, X-rays, gamma rays – you name it. I pump out this energy and it hurtles through space, crossing the 150 million km from me to Earth in just eight minutes, nineteen seconds flat. It smashes into that wet blanket, Atmosphere, driving moisture off land and sea to form fluffy Cloud. My energy heats the air, but unevenly, creating pressure differences that mix and churn up Atmosphere, so triggering Earth's wild weather.

● Surface temperature of the Sun: 5700 °C
● Highest recorded temperature on Earth: 57.8 °C (El Azizia, Libya, 1922)
● Sunniest place: Yuma, Arizona, USA (4000 hours of sunshine per year)

Sun

Seasons
■ World of Weather

✳ Four periods dividing the year – spring, summer, autumn, winter
✳ Each has its unique weather patterns and daylight hours
✳ Caused by changes in Earth's position in regard to the Sun

We're a wonky crew. It's our slant on life that makes spring change to summer and autumn to winter during the 12 months that Earth takes to race around Sun.

Earth's big round belly (the Equator) receives the greatest intensity of sunshine, because its surface is square on to hotshot Sun. Areas further away from the Equator get a more spread-out dose of Sun's energy, because the surface slopes away. At the same time, the Earth orbits Sun at an angle of 23.5°, which means one hemisphere is always receiving more direct energy than the other, and has summer, while the other is having winter. The fact that Earth's orbit is elliptical (oval-shaped), and not circular, only adds to this effect. All in all, it's thanks to us that you always know whether to wear a bobble hat or Bermudas!

● Summer solstice: the longest day of the year
● Winter solstice: the shortest day of the year
● Equinox: one of two days in the year when night and day are roughly equal

Seasons

Climate
World of Weather

☀ The typical weather for a region over a long period of time
☀ Affected by latitude, height and closeness to water
☀ Normally measured as an average of weather over 30 years

I'm The General, a grand planner poised over maps and charts. I'm not content to deal with the here and now, but take the long view. I present the bigger picture.

While weather is all about Atmosphere's activity at present – if it's sunny or raining, windy, cloudy or dry – I deal with the behaviour of the weather over time. I give a reliable picture of what the weather is like at any time of year, year after year. Sure, it might be raining now, but if soggy old Rain fails to show up for months on end, a place has a dry climate. I vary depending on many factors. For example, equatorial regions are hot because of the latitude, but may also be wet or dry. Oceans store and shift Sun's energy around the globe, so some areas are warmer than you might expect for their latitude – well, no one's perfect!

● Climate zones: tropical, monsoon, dry, warm, cool and cold
● World's wettest place: the Khasi Hills, India (about 12,000 mm rain per year)
● World's driest place: the Atacama Desert, Chile (less than 0.1 mm rain per year)

Climate

Monsoon

■ World of Weather

☀ A weather system of two seasons – rainy and dry
☀ Marked by a switch of wind direction and a change in rainfall
☀ Occurs in northern Australia, west Africa, south and east Asia

Boy, am I a big crybaby! Every year, I turn from bright and sunny to sullen and sulky. I turn on the tears, instantly bringing cloudbursts of my favourite play pal, Rain.

So, why am I so wet? Well, in winter, the sea stays warm for longer than the land does. The air overlying the land cools and sinks, creating a zone of high pressure, which drives winds from the land out across the sea. But in summer, the land heats up quicker than the sea and the cycle reverses. Now, as the warm air over land rises, it draws in water-laden air from the sea. This air rises, too, shedding my violent rain-bursts as it cools. I am a great provider of fresh water, vital for healthy crops. But I can also be deadly, dumping so much water onto the land that Flood shows up. The very thought brings me close to tears…

● First monsoon: about 15 to 20 million years ago
● Earth's wettest mountains: 3000 to 4000 mm of rain per year (Western Ghats, India)
● The summer monsoon accounts for over 80 % of India's annual rainfall

Monsoon

El Niño

World of Weather

* Upsets the normal interaction of the ocean and atmosphere
* Affects western coast of North, South and Central America
* El Niño is Spanish for "little boy"

I am your genuine tropical terror, a scamp that shows up every two to five years. I usually arrive around Christmas time, but I'm no welcome present, I can tell you!

I tamper with the normal conditions of the Pacific Ocean. What's normal, you say? Well, trade winds at the Equator push water westwards across the Pacific to Indonesia and Australia. Cold water rises up from the depths to replace the water shifted across the surface. With it come nutrients that make the East Pacific superb for fishing. Perfect… until I come along, that is. I weaken squally Wind, so breaking the cycle. The warm water stays where it is, and the cold water does not rise. The effects on Atmosphere can be devastating: Drought parches the west, Rain and Flood swamp the east, and there are fewer fish. I love chaos!

● Followed by La Niña, which reverses the conditions
● Upwelling: the movement of water from the depths of the ocean to its surface
● Average West Pacific sea level: 0.5 m higher than the East Pacific sea level

El Niño

Forecast

World of Weather

✳ This boffin uses scientific methods to predict the weather
✳ Has data-gatherers, such as satellites and weather balloons
✳ Supplies information to aviation, shipping and the military

Everyone's desperate to know what the weather's up to and I've got all the answers. Yup, I take real-time data from my vast team of gatherers, feed it into complex computer models and... hope for a reliable outlook. Hey, I'm dealing with nature here! I can be short-range (tomorrow) or long-range (a month). However, the longer the range, the less accurate I am. Bah!

Forecast

● First recorded forecasts: 650 BCE (Babylonian)
● A rapid fall in pressure signifies that bad weather is coming
● Rising pressure suggests that more settled weather can be expected

Weather Satellite

World of Weather

* Orbits Earth and is used to monitor the weather
* Reveals much about global weather and climate
* An early-warning system of climate change

Weather Satellite

I'm a space-age marvel, endlessly circling, always watching. I keep my fully automatic, unblinking eye on the weather. I monitor Wind shifting and Cloud forming. I zap data and pictures back to Earth for you to see on TV. But it's not all storms and clouds; I'm also something of a snitch when it comes to global warming. There's not much that vile Climate Change gets past me!

● Orbit height: 850 to 35,880 km
● The first-ever weather satellite, TIROS-1, was launched in 1960
● The Antarctic ozone hole was first observed by weather satellite in 1984

Climate Change
■ World of Weather

✳ Flame-haired character currently causing global warming
✳ A bringer of extreme weather, such as floods and droughts
✳ Your "carbon footprint" is your own personal contribution

Let's face it, Earth is getting hotter. A lot of this is down to me, but no matter how many times I say it, there are still *soooo* many people who refuse to believe that I exist.

"Even Climate admits to being a little unpredictable", they say, and "Climate's been warmer in the past you know". Yeah, right! I love you humans – there you go burning your fossil fuels (coal, oil, gas) and pumping your greenhouse gases into Atmosphere. Meanwhile that big stuffy blanket is getting horribly sticky with all that extra heat it's trapping. The ice caps and glaciers are melting and sea levels are rising. I'm just itching for it all to get out of hand. You could reduce your personal energy usage and shift to cleaner, greener ways of producing power. But, hey, who's listening to me? I don't exist, remember!

● Average global temperature rise: 0.8 °C since 1900
● Main greenhouse gases: water vapour, carbon dioxide, methane
● The 2000s were the hottest decade in 400 years

Climate Change

Chapter 2

■ Blue-sky Dreamers

These guys are all up in the air. They may seem a bunch of dizzy dreamers, but the stuff they get up to affects our day-to-day weather. Meet Atmosphere, enveloping Earth in its huge gassy blanket and playing host to all the Blue-sky dudes. You'll find Jet Stream whizzing around here, and Weather Front along for the ride. Cloud shows up when water vapour in the air reaches its dew point and forms liquid droplets. Things really get going when Wind blows in – you can *feel* Atmosphere then. Pressure's highs and lows reflect the shifting weight of Atmosphere's constantly moving gases, giving us clues as to what's coming up…

Atmosphere

Pressure

Wind

Jet Stream

Cloud

Weather Front

Atmosphere

■ Blue-sky Dreamers

☀ The stuff that the sky is made from
☀ A blanket of gases that keeps us warm
☀ Causes the weather by spreading heat and water about

If "party" and "atmosphere" are words you like, then look no further for the perfect host. Mine is a heady cocktail of four parts nitrogen to one part oxygen, with just a dash of argon. Life with me is a *gas*.

I'm an invisible marvel, wrapping around the world to keep it cosy and shielding life from a bombardment of lethal radiation from space. I have five layers. Rain, Hail, Cloud and Weather Front all strut their stuff in my lower layer, the troposphere. The ozone layer is found above that, in the stratosphere. Other gases spike my mix – nasty greenhouse gases that Climate Change brags about. They're present in tiny amounts, but boy are they trouble! Pollen, volcanic ash, dust and the pollutant sulphur dioxide also muscle their way in. It chokes me up to think about it.

● The layers: troposphere, stratosphere, mesosphere, thermosphere, exosphere
● Coldest part of the atmosphere: −100 °C (the mesosphere)
● Official boundary of Earth's atmosphere with space: 100 km up (Kármán line)

Atmosphere

Pressure

▪ Blue-sky Dreamers

✴ The weight of the gases in the atmosphere
✴ Measured using a barometer
✴ A change in pressure signals a shift in the weather

You've probably heard the expression "as light as air", but that's just the half of it. What goes up must come down, that's my motto. I'm an up-and-down sort of fella!

When people talk about me, they mean the weight of all the air over an area of land or sea. Imagine a tall column of air rising up into the sky. The higher you get in the column, the less air there is above you, pressing down. This is why the pressure drops when you rise in an aeroplane or climb a mountain. Atmosphere's gases are constantly shifting and I change with them. I have highs and lows, but they are not like your uplifting highs and heavy, heavy lows. Instead, air sinks over an area of land with high pressure, while low pressure makes the opposite happen – it causes the air to rise. Up, up and away...

● Average sea-level pressure: 101.325 kPa (kilopascals)
● Highest recorded atmospheric pressure: 108.57 kPa (Mongolia, 2001)
● Lowest recorded: 85 kPa, in the centre of a tornado (South Dakota, USA, 2003)

Pressure

Wind

■ Blue-sky Dreamers

☀ Huffs and puffs to move air masses about
☀ Blows from high-pressure zones to low-pressure zones
☀ Winds that blow most of the time are called trade winds

I like to get things movin'. I wanna see trees dancin' and hats a-tumblin'. I can be very slight – a breath of air – and I can rage. My storm force whips tiles off roofs, flings cars about and snaps branches. When I blow, you feel Atmosphere press against you. And because I shift air about, I also move water and heat. Temperatures feel lower than they actually are when I'm around. *Brrr!*

Wind

● Trade winds: steady easterly winds that blow across the Earth's tropical oceans
● World's windiest place: Commonwealth Bay, Antarctica (up to 322 km/h)
● Highest recorded cyclonic wind speed: 408 km/h (Barrow Island, Australia, 1996)

Jet Stream

Blue-sky Dreamers ■

* ☀ This high-altitude, high-speed wind usually flows east
* ☀ Found around Earth's poles and subtropical regions
* ☀ Can create a weather front and drive it forward

Jet Stream

Chocks away! Strap on those flying goggles, and follow my narrow currents as they snake around the Earth at high speed. Isn't it every guy's fantasy to fly with the real jets in the cool stratosphere, way above the planet? Well, I'm up there, baby, looking down on my fellow Blue-sky pals. You don't want to mess with me, though. Planes that go against my flow could suffer delays!

* ● Jet-stream height: 7 to12 km (polar jets); 10 to16 km (subtropical jets)
* ● Typical size of jet stream: few hundred km wide; 5 km deep
* ● Jet-stream speed: 200 to 400 km/h

Cloud

■ Blue-sky Dreamers

- ✳ Large collection of water droplets or ice crystals in the sky
- ✳ Occurs when air cools and water vapour turns to liquid
- ✳ One of the best indicators of weather to come

Wandering high and lonely, I'm a dreamy fellow. Poets and folk who stare at the sky go all wishy-washy about me, but there's more to me than my soft, pillowy looks.

In fact, I'm rather grey and damp – a mass of swirling water vapour. My different forms are classed by shape and height in Atmosphere's lowest level, the troposphere, which is where I hang out. Wispy cirrus floats its boat very high up and, coming down to Earth, you'll find puffy white cumulus, greying alto types, blanket-like stratus and rain-bearing nimbus. My forms often combine: stratocumulus is the round, grey-hulled cloud you get on a cloudy-with-sunny-patches kind of day, while nimbo-stratus is dark and leaden. If you see me getting lower in the sky, Weather Front is on its way. Run for cover!

- ● Inventor of cloud classification: Luke Howard (1803)
- ● Amount of Earth's water in clouds: 0.035 %
- ● Aeroplanes that fly through clouds often experience turbulence

Cloud

Weather Front

■ Blue-sky Dreamers

☀ This bad boy brings a change in the wind and weather
☀ Happens when cold and warm air masses meet
☀ Passes overhead in 24 hours and keeps moving for days

I'm a pushy little fella that comes about when two air masses meet but refuse to mingle. Say they have a different density (one is lighter than the other) – they jostle and circle each other, but never mix.

I create a boundary between a cold air mass and a warm one whenever one approaches the other. A heavy, cold air mass will undercut a warm one, barging through to get ahead, while a lighter, warm air mass simply sits on top of a cold one, forcing it out of the way. I can last for days as they battle it out, each drawing in fresh supplies, and I take my direction from speedy Jet Stream. It's at times like these that you'll find the weather happening. Wind, Cloud, Rain, Snow, Tornado and Thunderstorm all try to get a look in if they can. They've got some "front"!

● Warm front on a weather map: red semicircles
● Cold front on a weather map: blue triangles
● Occluded front: when a warm front meets a cold one

Weather Front

Chapter 3

■ Wet 'n' Wild

Here we have a pretty steamy bunch, the Wet 'n' Wild members of the weather world. They all have something to do with the way in which air holds water vapour. You already know that warm air holds more water vapour than cold air. You also know that warm air rises, but here's the rub: as a mass of warm air rises, it cools down. Its vapour condenses (turns into liquid water), which then falls back down to Earth as precipitation. What you need to worry about is whether it falls as a liquid (Rain) or a solid (Snow and Hail). Either way, you'd better look out, because you're likely to get soaking wet, freezing cold or both!

Rain

Snow

Hail

Fog

Frost

Rainbow

Rain
■ Wet 'n' Wild

✳ Liquid precipitation that causes blue feelings and worse…
✳ Made when air holding water vapour cools
✳ A raindrop is shaped more like a burger bun than a teardrop

People treat me like I'm some kind of a party pooper. The moment I gather, all grey and cloudy above their heads, I hear nothing but moaning and groaning. What a bunch of washouts! You know better than that, I'm sure. You know that I bring much needed water to the land, and that Earth rejoices at my arrival.

I tumble out of Cloud when water droplets or ice crystals get too heavy to hang suspended in the air. It all starts with the rising of warm air and its vapour, which turns from gas to liquid as it rises. But lovely Cloud has told you this already! If it gets colder, the water droplets emerging from the air start to clump together. If it's really cold (as it often is), ice crystals form. Soon poor Cloud bursts and I drop all the way back to Earth, melting as I fall. Splish splash!

● Speed of falling rain: up to 18 km/h
● Global average annual rainfall: 990 mm
● Most rain in one day: 1778 mm (La Réunion, Indian Ocean, 1952)

Rain

Snow
■ Wet 'n' Wild

❉ Solid, icy precipitation; individual crystals of frozen water
❉ This beauty comes in many shapes and sizes
❉ Can be dry or wet, depending on air temperature

Everyone loves ME! Delicate and oh-so pretty, I'm "snow" much fun to play in. Next time you make a snowball, just think – no two flakes of mine are the same. Incredible but true: each of the millions and billions of snowflakes lying about and falling from the sky is as individual as you!

You'd better wrap up warm when I'm swirling about. I'm the chilly stuff that happens when Rain doesn't quite manage to melt on its way down from Cloud. Since I am made of individual ice crystals, I am extremely light and fluffy. Gusty Wind whisks me hither and thither, building me up in drifts in sheltered corners where I come to rest. The air spaces between my crystals compress when you walk on a bed of me, which makes me squeak and creak. Cute? Heck yes, but a heavy fall of me causes havoc!

● Average speed of falling snow: 1 m/s
● Largest snowfall (1 storm): 480 cm (Mount Shasta Ski Bowl, California, USA, 1959)
● Number of words for snow in the Saami languages of northern Europe: 300

Snow

Hail

■ Wet 'n' Wild

☀ Extreme form of solid precipitation; frozen balls of ice
☀ Formed in cold cumulonimbus storm clouds
☀ Collisions in clouds build up static electricity to make lightning

A real bruiser, I hammer on roofs and strip crops bare. I form in tall storm clouds, where strong updraughts shoot water droplets up into the air. Layers of ice build around each drop, and so I am born! Up, up I go, growing bigger and meaner with each new coat of ice. Once I'm too heavy for the updraught to support me, I plummet all the way down to Earth… and destruction.

Hail

● Hailstone size: 0.5 to 15 cm
● Hailstone speed (a hailstone of 1 cm): 9 m/s
● World's heaviest hailstone: 1 kg (Gopalganj, Bangladesh, 1986)

Fog

Wet 'n' Wild ▪

* ❋ Ground-hugging cloud and close cousin of mist and smog
* ❋ Forms when cold air is trapped beneath a warm air mass
* ❋ Disappears in the blink of an eye when things heat up

Fog

I'm a wet blanket! I love to wrap things in my damp embrace. You'll find me lurking wherever water-vapour-laden warm air hits a chilly spot. Cooling rapidly, vapour condenses out of the air as millions of tiny droplets of dangling liquid water, aka me, Fog. I love to torment drivers, pilots and ships' captains, literally blinding them with my mysterious misty looks. So who's wet now!

* ● Official definition: when visibility is reduced to less than 1 km
* ● World's foggiest place: Grand Banks, Newfoundland, Canada
* ● Water content: less than 1 litre in 1 km³ of fog

Frost

Wet 'n' Wild

- ☀ Ice that forms at ground level, made from frozen dew
- ☀ Occurs when the land is colder than the air
- ☀ This wintry fellow kills off plants

Cold and cruel, I creep around the place in the night, freezing the ground, cars, trees, windows and roofs with my icy touch. My sharp nip can mean death to many a plant hanging on to life as autumn turns. And I'll bite any veggies silly enough to start growing too early in spring.

It takes a special kind of magic to bring me out. When fiery Sun sets, the ground quickly loses the heat of the day. Water vapour in the warm air condenses out on contact with the cold land and dewdrops appear. If it is below freezing, this dew forms chilly old me – glistening ice crystals that coat any surface upon which they land. Depending on the conditions, I appear in different guises. As hoar frost, I occur on particularly chilly nights. I'm so white and thick, you might think I'm that flake, Snow.

- ● Slight frost: 0 to –3.5 ° C
- ● Moderate frost: –3.6 to –6.5 ° C
- ● Severe frost: –6.6 to –11.5 ° C

Frost

Rainbow

■ Wet 'n' Wild

✳ A curving band of colour in the sky, found opposite the Sun
✳ Occurs when light shines through droplets of water in the air
✳ Often seen in the spray coming from waves or waterfalls

Mine is a multicoloured magic that brings a smile to your face. My looping bands of bright colour are made by two bittersweet pals of mine – Rain and Sun.

My hero, Isaac Newton, was the genius who discovered how I came to exist, and why my lovely colours always appear in the same order. You see, when light enters a drop of rain, it slows down just enough for the different frequencies bundled up inside white light to split. The light bounces off the back of the raindrop, and is reflected in all its glory as red, orange, yellow, green, blue, indigo and violet. Because I'm a purely optical phenomenon, you can chase me, but you'll never find the point at which I touch the ground – the rainbow's end. I'm afraid the same can be said about that pot of gold. It just ain't there!

● Longest-lasting rainbow: 3 hours (Gwynedd, UK, 1979)
● Memory aid for rainbow colours: ROY G-BIV
● Angle of reflection inside a raindrop: 40 to 42°

Rainbow

Chapter 4
Extreme Weather

Be wary of this wild bunch! A group of freak weather conditions, these characters have a mean streak a mile wide. They are awesomely powerful – without so much as breaking a sweat, they can swat cars, sweep away roads and bridges and make matchsticks out of houses. Normally, you barely feel the weight of the air, but this lot show you exactly the punch that Atmosphere can pull when it's stirred up. Scientists worry that global warming is making this lot more common. And while they are certainly breathtaking to behold, let's be thankful they don't come knocking more often... for now!

Thunderstorm

Lightning

Hurricane

Tornado

Ice Storm

Flood

Drought

Thunderstorm

■ Extreme Weather

☀ Booming bruiser that brings rain, hail, lightning and thunder
☀ Formed in tall, anvil-shaped cumulonimbus clouds
☀ Thunder is a shockwave that rumbles out after a lightning bolt

Full of boisterous bluster, I bring strong winds and wild weather. There's not a day goes by without me bursting my seams above some place or other on this planet.

I'm most likely to occur on hot, humid days, when warm, moist air surges upwards into the sky. In the same way that Cloud comes about, the warm air cools and the water vapour turns into liquid. But updraughts keep my clouds building up until they are monsters, sometimes over 20 km high! So strong are the updraughts that they shoot moisture-laden air right to the top of the troposphere, where it flattens out and forms my ominous anvil shape. Well, I can only take so much, and it is simply a matter of time before I start lashing Rain down and flashing Lightning! Hey, don't blame me – it's lonely up there!

● Number of thunderstorms happening right now: about 1800
● Height of a typical thundercloud: 8 to 10 km
● Distance in km: number of seconds between lightning and thunder divided by 3

Thunderstorm

Lightning
■ Extreme Weather

✳ Sudden burst of electricity from the clouds
✳ Can be sheet (cloud-to-cloud) or forked (cloud-to-ground)
✳ Always takes the quickest route to Earth

I'm a real flash dude! I light up the sky with my electric moves. My bolts heat air about three times hotter than Sun's surface. The energy released in just one bolt is enough to toast about 100,000 slices of bread. Cooking!

I thrive on Thunderstorm's turbulence. Water droplets, ice crystals and dust bump and jostle in the updraughts and downdraughts to create a static charge. I can equalize the charge by leaping between clouds as sheet lightning. But sometimes I discharge to the ground. First, I send out a negatively charged streamer of electrically charged air. This encourages a positively charged feeler to rise up from any high point on Earth. As soon as the two connect, I discharge with full force. This return stroke is what you see as lightning. I'm one sparky guy, I tell you!

● Lightning bolt speed: 220,000 km/h
● Heat of air around a lightning bolt: 30,000 °C
● Average number of lightning storms, globally: 16 million per year

Lightning

Hurricane

■ Extreme Weather

- ☀ Weather system that brings strong winds and very heavy rain
- ☀ The centre, or eye, of a hurricane is very low in pressure
- ☀ Aka tropical cyclone and typhoon

Brooding and sulking, I'm an angry tiger of moist air, chasing my tail. Self-pitying Thunderstorm is a mere cub compared to me. My might is truly awesome! Mwoahaha!

I form out at sea when Sun evaporates colossal quantities of water off the surface. The rising air and condensing water vapour build up an enormous swirling heat engine that spirals anticlockwise in the northern hemisphere and clockwise in the southern hemisphere. Driven by Earth's rotation and steering winds, I set off on my trail of wild destruction – my eye calm and warm, yet surrounded by great walls of menacing cloud. Round and round I go, causing havoc and uprooting anything in my path. Fellow extremist, Flood, bursts forth from my heavy rains and storm surges to maximize my terrifying potential for disaster.

- ● Deadliest hurricane: over 300,000 killed (Bhola cyclone, Bangladesh, 1970)
- ● Strongest hurricane: 310 km/h wind speeds (Typhoon Tip, Pacific Ocean, 1979)
- ● Longest-lasting hurricane: 31 days (Hurricane John, Pacific Ocean, 1994)

Hurricane

Tornado
■ Extreme Weather

☀ A spinning tube of air, its wind speed is impossible to measure
☀ Reaches down from a thundercloud to the ground
☀ Travels an unpredictable path, creating chaos

C'mon everybody, let's do the twist! I love to dance and I long to pick you up and spin you around. But, to be honest, I know I'll just trash the place!

Responsible for some of the highest wind speeds on Earth, I'm about as extreme as weather gets. Coming out from the bottom of a cumulonimbus thundercloud, I hit the ground running, tossing cars about willy-nilly and smashing up houses. When I cross water, I suck it up into huge towers called waterspouts. (I've been known to make it rain frogs and fish!) I often take a turn in Tornado Alley in the USA, between the Rocky and Appalachian Mountains. Most days, I run out of puff quickly, but every now and then I get on a roll. The 2011 Super Outbreak made as many as 322 tornadoes in three days. Blow me!

● Longest tornado travel: 352 km (Tri-State Tornado, USA, 1925)
● Longest tornado duration: about 3.5 hours (Tri-State Tornado, USA, 1925)
● Fastest forward speed: 117 km/h (Tri-State Tornado, USA, 1925)

Tornado

Ice Storm
■ Extreme Weather

☀ This malign pixie coats all surfaces in thick, slippery ice
☀ Strikes with hardly any warning when the conditions are right
☀ Also known as a glaze event and silver thaw

Merciless and mean, I freeze all that I touch. I love to cause utter mayhem, pulling down power lines and creating multi-car pile-ups with my hard, icy glaze.

I'm a pretty rare event, although I seem to be occuring more frequently. It takes a certain kind of weather to bring me about: something I call an airy sandwich – a warm-air filling squished between two cold-air bread slices. Snow falling from the cold top layer melts as it passes through the warm middle part and then cools again as it falls through the cold bottom layer. Drops that don't turn to ice hit the already-frozen surface as supercooled water (below freezing point, but not yet solid). The second they land, they solidify into hard ice, crusting heavily on power lines, pylons, roads, houses and cars. Ice, ice, baby!

● Official ice-storm definition: 0.64 cm of ice on exposed surfaces
● Power-line strain: 0.6 cm of ice adds about 225 kg per line span
● Worst ice storm: 20 cm of ice (Idaho, USA, 1961)

Ice Storm

Flood

■ Extreme Weather

* ☀ Water overflow that damages buildings, roads and sewers
* ☀ This big drip has devastating effects on low-lying areas
* ☀ Dependent on rainfall, storms and climate

A soggy surplus of the wet stuff, I turn up when water bursts out of its normal channels. Fluid, creeping and dangerous, my sudden, fast-flowing, evil currents sweep people off their feet and away. I adore Hurricane's storm surges and the heavy rains that make rivers swell. Best of all, I love to catch the Earth unawares; I flash across the land before it has time to soak me up.

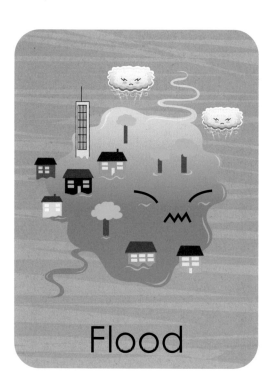

Flood

* ● Deadliest flood: 2,500,000 to 3,700,000 killed (Yellow River, China, 1931)
* ● World's largest flood defences: the Netherlands
* ● Definition of a flash flood: occurs within a timescale of less than 6 hours

Drought
Extreme Weather ■

* Extended dry period without rain; often causes crops to fail
* Brought on by climate in dry regions (e.g. the Horn of Africa)
* Can lead to deforestation, erosion and desertification

Drought

I am ying to Flood's yang. A sustained period of fine weather, I might sound promising but don't be fooled. I bring terrible dry spells that parch the land. Believe me, life without water is unpleasant. Vital crops and livestock perish and starvation looms. And once I'm in, I'm hard to shift: I drive moisture from the ground, leaving not a drop to supply fresh rainfall. It's thirsty work!

● Deadliest drought: an estimated 9,000,000 deaths (China 1876–79)
● Proportion of Earth's land surface that is dry land: 41 %
● Area affected by American "Dust Bowl" drought (1930–36): 400,000 km^2

Index

Character entries are **bold**

A
air masses 28, 32, 34, 41, 62
altitude 29, 62
Atmosphere 8, 12, 16, 20, 22, **24**, 26, 28, 30, 46
autumn 10, 42
axis 8, 62, 63

C
carbon footprints 20, 62
Climate 4, 8, **12**, 19, 20, 58, 59
Climate Change 19, **20**, 24
Cloud 8, 12, 14, 19, 22, 24, **30**, 32, 36, 38, 40, 41, 48, 50, 52, 54

D
deforestation 59, 62
desertification 59, 62
downdraughts 50, 62
Drought 16, 20, **59**

E
Earth 6, 8, 10, 19, 20, 22, 24, 28, 29, 30, 34, 36, 40, 48, 50, 52, 54, 58, 59
El Niño 6, **16**, 63

Equator 10, 12, 16, 62
erosion 59, 62

F
Flood 14, 16, 20, 52, **58**, 59
Fog **41**
Forecast 4, **18**
frequency 44, 63, 64
Frost **42**

G
gamma rays 8, 63, 64
global warming 19, 20, 46
greenhouse gases 20, 24, 63

H
Hail 24, 34, **40**, 48
hemispheres 10, 52, 63
Hurricane **52**, 58

I
Ice Storm **56**
infrared waves 8, 63

JL
Jet Stream 22, **29**, 32
La Niña 16, 63
latitude 12, 63
Lightning 40, 48, **50**

MN

Monsoon 6, 12, **14**
Newton, Isaac 44

O

orbits 6, 10, 19, 63
ozone 24, 63, 64
ozone hole 63

P

poles 6, 29, 63
precipitation 34, 36, 38, 40, 63
Pressure 8, 14, 18, 22, **26**, 28, 52

R

radio waves 8, 64
Rain 12, 14, 16, 24, 30, 32, 34, **36**, 38, 44, 48, 52, 54, 58, 59
Rainbow **44**, 64

S

Seasons 6, **10**
Snow 32, 34, **38**, 42, 56
Solar System 8, 64
spring 10, 42
storms 28, 32, 40, 50, 52, 56, 58

storm surges 52, 58, 64
subtropical 29, 64
summer 6, 10, 14
Sun 6, **8**, 10, 12, 42, 44, 50, 52

T

thunder 48, 54
Thunderstorm 32, **48**, 50, 52
Tornado 32, **54**
trade winds 16, 28
tropical 12, 16, 28, 52, 64

UV

ultraviolet waves 8, 64
updraughts 40, 48, 50, 64
visible light 8, 64

W

Weather Front 22, 24, 29, 30, **32**
Weather Satellite 18, **19**
weather systems 6, 52
white light 44, 64
Wind 12, 14, 16, 19, 22, **28**, 29, 32, 38, 48, 52, 54
winter 6, 10, 14

X

X-rays 8, 64

Glossary

Air mass A vast body of air of one density (that is, at the same temperature and with the same water vapour content). When two air masses of different density meet they do not mix, but form a weather front.

Altitude Height above sea level.

Axis An imaginary line around which things rotate. Earth spins around an axis that connects the two poles.

Carbon footprint The amount of carbon released into the atmosphere as a result of an activity or process; a figure used to compare the energy consumed to make or do something.

Cyclonic When wind travels in a fluid circular motion, rotating in the same direction as Earth.

Deforestation The felling of trees and changing of forest land into farmland or an urban zone.

Density Mass per unit volume; normally the amount of material in a given chunk of stuff.

Desertification The changing of land into dry land, often the result of climate change or through overfarming.

Downdraught Air moving vertically downwards; descending air currents within clouds and areas of low pressure.

Equator An imaginary line around Earth, equidistant from North and South Poles and perpendicular to Earth's axis.

Erosion The wearing away of land by water, wind and other natural processes.

Frequency The rate at which something repeats itself; the number of cycles it makes per second. The different colours found in white light are made of light waves of different frequencies.

Gamma rays Electromagnetic radiation of very high frequency (higher frequency than X-rays).

Greenhouse gas Any gas in the atmosphere that traps infrared waves and stops them escaping Earth.

Hemisphere Half of the Earth; divided into northern and southern halves by the Equator.

Infrared waves Low-frequency electromagnetic radiation, felt as heat.

La Niña A weather phenomenon in the Pacific Ocean that has the reverse effects to El Niño.

Latitude Imaginary lines around the Earth, parallel to the Equator. High latitudes are near the poles, low latitudes are near the Equator.

Orbit The curved path of a planet around the Sun or a satellite around the Earth.

Ozone hole Where the ozone layer in Earth's atmosphere becomes depleted owing to the effects of pollution.

Poles The two fixed points on Earth's surface where its axis intersects with the surface. The North Pole is the furthest point north and the South Pole the furthest south on Earth.

Precipitation Water that falls to Earth from the sky as rain, snow, sleet or hail.

Glossary

Radiation Energy that travels as electromagnetic waves through space.

Radio waves Very low frequency electromagnetic radiation; can be generated by lightning.

Solar System The family of planets, asteroids and comets orbiting the Sun.

Storm surge When atmospheric pressure causes sea levels to rise during a storm.

Subtropical Relating to the regions next to the tropics. Climate is milder here than in the tropics, with hot summers but cooler winters.

Tropical The regions around the Equator, which mostly have a hot and humid climate, but can also be arid.

Ultraviolet waves Mid-frequency electromagnetic radiation that has a higher frequency than light. Ultraviolet waves can cause sunburn.

Updraught Air moving vertically upwards; rising currents within clouds and areas of high pressure.

Visible light Mid-frequency electromagnetic radiation, which the human eye can see.

White light Blended colours (frequencies) of light are perceived as white. It can be split by water droplets to form a seven-coloured rainbow.

X-rays High-frequency electromagnetic radiation – higher frequency than ultraviolet waves, but lower than gamma rays.